Prairie Schooner Book Prize in Poetry

EDITOR · Kwame Dawes

LUISA MURADYAN

AMEЯICAN
RADIAИCE

UNIVERSITY OF NEBRASKA
PRESS · LINCOLN AND LONDON

Library of Congress
Cataloging-in-Publication Data
Names: Muradyan, Luisa, author.
Title: American radiance /
Luisa Muradyan.
Description: Lincoln: University of
Nebraska Press, 2018. | Series: Prairie
schooner book prize in poetry
Identifiers: LCCN 2017056792
ISBN 9781496207753 (pbk.: alk. paper)
ISBN 9781496210920 (epub)
ISBN 9781496210937 (mobi)
ISBN 9781496210944 (pdf)
Classification: LCC PS3613.U693815 A6 2018
DDC 811/.6—dc23 LC record available
at https://lccn.loc.gov/2017056792

Set in Arno by Mikala R Kolander.
Designed by N. Putens.

For my family

Contents

Acknowledgments

Thank you to the editors of the journals below, where many of these poems first appeared, sometimes with different titles and in slightly altered form:

A-Minor Magazine: "This Was His Garden," "In the Moonlight"

anderbo: "Boot"

Blackbird: "Firefly," "Anecdote"

Camroc Press Review: "Records of Failed Weapons of World War II"

The Los Angeles Review: "7:40"

Mudlark: "Poem for the Man Playing Piano in Front of the Wall of Police"

Neon Literary Magazine: "The Seduction of Masha by Rasputin"

Ninth Letter: "Message from a Peeping Tom"

PANK: "If You Were Wondering about the Couple Who Owns the Funeral Home," "Translating Ashes," "Rumi in the Mouth of the Snake," "What Is True for Birds"

The Paris-American: "The Red Forest, Рыжий лес," "Crane"

Poetry International: "Clams," "Marriage," "Raptor"

Rattle Poets Respond: "Purple Rain"

West Branch: "American Radiance," "Adoration," "Crane Fly"

I am incredibly thankful for all of the wonderful people who have helped me bring this book into existence. To my family, friends, collaborators, and mentors—I could not have done this without your support. To my husband and son, thank you for being such an amazing source of love and joy every single day and for your constant encouragement. To my parents, thank you for always believing in my work and for giving me the strength to believe in myself. A special thank you to my writing mentor Kathleen Pierce, a true inspiration whom I am lucky to call my friend. Enormous thanks to the amazing Kwame Dawes—it has been an honor to work with you and the awesome *Prairie Schooner* team. Thanks also to the University of Nebraska Press, the University of Houston creative writing program, and Inprint. Thanks to my writing teachers Cyrus Cassells, Kevin Prufer, Roberto Tejada, Tony Hoagland, Martha Serpas, Nick Flynn, Tomas Morin, and Roger Jones. And thanks to my wonderful colleagues, classmates, and friends who spent time with this book before it was ever a book: Kayla Klein, Stephanie Motz, John Andrews, Mary Self, Elizabeth Zaleski, Courtney Ochsner, Ashley Strosnider, Denise Rodriguez, James Knippen, Carly Joy Miller, John Fry, Andi Boyd, Shiloh Booker, Nick Courtright, Kyle McCord, Georgia Pearle, Michele Nereim, and Erika Jo Brown.

AMERICAN RADIANCE

PART 1

Psalm for Odessa

If You Were Wondering about the Couple
Who Owns the Funeral Home

This isn't an erotic poem.
We are just two erotic people
sitting in the bathtub,
washing the dirt off each other's backs.
It's Tuesday, and on Tuesdays
we take inventory,
count the bodies in different orders,
and make up beautiful pie charts
to stay sane. Violet means these bodies
just got here and haven't even taken their shoes off.
Yellow means we just need to get them
up and around, put a little Miles Davis on.
Green means we are feeling young and
you're dancing like a dandelion again.
Blue means the blood hasn't left the body
yet, and you're a duchess in a room fit for a duchess,
the throne of formaldehyde. We spray perfume
on the bodies, we call that rose. Red is the hardest
color of all, it is the day we think of fire. Gray is
the morning after. We sweep it into porcelain jugs.
People say that the void is indescribable, but I tell you
it is brown and lacquer sitting on your mantle beneath
the portrait of your aunt Libby holding her tiny black dog.

Schwarzenegger in Prayer

There's a scene in *Predator*
where Arnold Schwarzenegger slaps the hand
of Carl Weathers and the camera focuses
for a moment
on the flex of their palms
and I think *this is how prayer works.*
Two tulips brush against each other in the rain
and when I watch action movies I believe
there is a reason Bruce Willis
can jump out of a helicopter
and propel into a circus tent, that perhaps
Yippee-ki-yay is really
another way to say *Baruch ata Adonai,*
that perhaps the choppa is a temple,
and when he says *Get to da choppa*
this is the call to return or just a call
to stand in the garden and marvel at the beauty
of wet flowers.

Purple Rain

After Purple Rain

In the Talmud there is an angel
whispering to every blade of grass: grow, grow.
In the other world, Prince whispers to every dove: cry, cry,
and when they asked me about the status of my searching
I nodded and told him I had been purified
in the waters of Lake Minnetonka.
Here's the thing about wearing a blouse—
you put it on one sleeve at a time,
become a man one silver hoop earring
at a time. I've never understood why
God gave us five fingers on each hand
when I would have made do with two.
Those were the fingers with which you
touched my outstretched hand
when I was made into a woman,
the ceiling of the Sistine chapel
painted with your raspberry tongue.

Clams

You say don't use words like *sad* in poetry
but I am as sad as a sad cloud crying
at a sad cloud convention.
If sadness were a fruit
it would be a sadberry
which is related to the blueberry
but sadder. And if sad were a type
of dinosaur it would be all dinosaurs
because the Sadasorous Rex and all
his friends are dead. And when you go
to a sadness party in your mock turtleneck
it's really just an old man watching the finale
of *The Bachelor* by himself, and when I say
watching the finale of *The Bachelor* I mean you're
in an alleyway watching feral cats fight over
an empty box of pizza.
Or maybe I've gotten it wrong
and when I say a phrase like *I'm sad*
I have no idea what that means,
because *abstraction is the failure of language.*
But wouldn't it be great if when I say
I'm as happy as a clam, there really is something
beyond a bivalve mollusk burying his body
into the sediment. The day at the beach
when we dug up so many clams
they ate through the plastic bag and spilled
across the sand like pebbles.

Bruce Willis, in the Light

I believe that we all die hard.
There is no gentle light,
only the rage of the butterfly
who is capable of great fury
but sweetly named after the churn
of milk and flight. I was named for
my grandmother, and I carry
her anger in this life and the next.
Beautiful Bruce Willis
whose wings are covered in shrapnel,
save me from these sequels,
suspend me in the disbelief
of the afterlife. Carry me away
from the multiple car explosion
in slow motion, with a predictable
soundtrack. Crawling with me
through the air vent, looking
for a way to breath.

Macho Man Randy Savage

First Thanksgiving, 1991

Ten dollars will get you
a bottle of vodka,
but a bottle of rubbing
alcohol is 99 cents,
so we set the table
and give thanks, the World
Wrestling Federation on
in the background and
our drunk neighbor
poised like a walrus
on the kitchen countertop,
teeth shinning, whiskers
long and pointed. Arms
raised like Macho Man Randy
Savage and falling
from his podium. Jaw
shattered like crystal,
teeth scattered on the
linoleum floor, and the glow
of pink tassels. My aunt
hysterical. The sound
of OOOOH YEEEAH!
coming from the television.

7:40

My students complain when I choose the music
for Classy Music Mondays, and I sway them
with endearing catchphrases like *I'll be Bach*,
but even then I wonder about the fuss of an aria
or the humor behind a sonata or what kind of instrument
I would turn myself into. The truth is
I'd like to be a piccolo or a French horn
but I've lived my life as a trombone
and I was raised by a drum. My mother banging her hand
on the table begging the Kansas String Band
to learn the 7:40, a popular Jewish folk song
from Odessa. The song that even my parents danced to
at their Soviet wedding, where God was not allowed,
only invoked among the pickled tomatoes,
a song that was sung every evening before 8 p.m.,
every evening as Jews all over the city rushed
to the last train out of Odessa.
7:10 the sun begins to fade 7:20 our goods are packed
7:30 warm up the band 7:40 our legs are running
7:40 I'm singing songs 7:40 we are packed like rats in train cars
7:40 we dance in a circle 7:40 my mother is slapped in school
7:40 my mother changes her name 7:40 I marry a gentile
7:40 don't tell them who or what you are
7:40 a trombone 7:40 I'm screaming like a train
7:40 who comes for me at the end of the night
7:40 what is the difference between a song and a scream
7:40 the conductor is nowhere to be found
7:40 look how joyfully we disappear

Prodigal Son

There is a hole in my bathtub
where ants trickle in
and I remember the sugar
ants in my grandfather's kitchen
dancing as if they were without
bodies or mandibles, me slicing
lemons and sprinkling them
with sugar, ants drowning
in my cup, drinking my tea
in silence not wanting to tell
my blind grandfather
that he lived in a house of ants
and that it was actually
thousands of ants
moving in one body
helping him button his shirt
or pulling the blankets
over him at night.

Reader, my grandfather did not die.
He simply became less man and more
ant, less misery and more shadow.
Waiting for his son who would never
come back. Where there were once eyes—

ants rotating like obsidian
clusters of stars.
Where there was once memory—
tunnels dug through dirt,
dust swept out of his chest.

Reader, remember
ants can be destroyed,
a house can be absolved,
but who will hold you
when the memories swarm back?

That day you found out
you would become
a father, heart beating
inside a poppy seed
no bigger than an ant.

Lilies

My mother brought with her
mostly sentimental things
from the Soviet Union.
Things given on her wedding day:

empty locket, broken watch,
lily-lipped teapot,
crown of dried lilies,
linen dress for wedding,
linen sheet for sleeping,
linen sheet previously blessed
for procreation,
bottle of lily perfume that broke
in the crate, lily-scented wool
blanket covered in broken glass,
lily-perfume-stained photographs
of all dead relatives, journal where
her mother kept track
of those who were murdered
in a field of lilies, notes
from the state, chain-link necklace
dug out of the dirt, paperwork
for food, paperwork for paper, paper
with forbidden writing, pages filled
with pictures of lilies my mother drew
in the interrogation room with lily wallpaper.

My mother who hates lilies.

Maria Rasputin

My father was a saint. I loved him
the way all of the children of saints do,
bowed down and speechless.

Whatever they said about my father
I will remember him beautiful like this—
eye sockets full of fireflies

making up psalms for the centipedes. *Blessed*
are your many legs, blessed are the limbs of your desire.
Blessed are the meek, for they shall inherit the silence.

Why do we even call them legs?
To a centipede it could be an arm.
Mashenka, today I teach you about silence.

Ripped out like a turnip he proved his point.
My father was never silent his entire life.
When they found him dead in the Neva

I heard him howling, *Mashenka, the meekness!*
Maybe silence was just another way
to refer to all of the music we did not hear.

If I had been born anything other than a woman
I could have had a thousand ears.
I could have heard how the silence bends
into the appendages of the night.

The Red Forest, Рыжий лес

Wolf spider teach me to be invisible
that I may pray teeth first,
mouth full of flies. The forest body
overgrown with wild tomatoes—
nuclear garden, electric mausoleum.
My mother in her pregnancy did not know
that I had sprouted a tail and two
extra fingers or needles that thread
golden webs. This forest full
of unclaimed scarves and sick
stories that thousands of years later
will be called fables. When Ivan exploded
his nuclear body the heroine gave birth
to the many limbs of time. Religion, I return,
wolf spider, let me in.

Crane

The morning almost too white,
I look down and continue peeling plums.
My grandfather dead but not quiet.
The sound of mourning rising and falling,
my grandmother calling all the birds
in Texas by their Ukrainian names,
kran, vorona, shulika.
Our birdhouse overcrowded with
ghosts who push out the hummingbirds
and sing such strange music.

Resurrection

For Leonard Baskin

My fallen and risen Christ,
was it man who made
the first metal bird
or was it bird
who made the first man flesh?
Ripping off his feathers
and then erupting in Rapture.

Rupture is an important word—
her genital-less body shoved
head first into the easy bake oven.
I tried to find one that looked like you.
She had my dark hair.

Insanity is what killed the dinosaurs,
the psalms written first with teeth
and then tail. Ten pterodactyl
commandments, all ending in flight.

Inheritance—
my grandmother was burned alive.
Let me repeat that.

It took a long time for man to figure out
how to fly. On power lines,
resurrected women everywhere.

The Seduction of Masha by Rasputin

Take this old
and tangled beard
woven by spiders.
I found you years ago
in that gooseberry bush,
naked legs; you were
just a child making up stories
for the insects. You pretended
you were a goddess,
fire ants in your hair, your face
covered in flames, your mouth
full of gooseberries.
Just a little carnation then,
caterpillar with two legs.
Let us play chess
the way the angels do,
without consequences or bodies.
You see it's not easy speaking to God,
he's too busy watching the snow fall
through the corridor
and only hears his own name.
So say it repeatedly. Scream it
as many times as you want,
glorious God, God almighty,
oh, God of the insects.

Doves

For Isaac Babel

I wouldn't know that I was a Jew
if I hadn't been told
on every corner of Odessa, but I believe
this is what it is like to be a dove.
With your red mouth and white neck
always hungry, always looking for seeds.
And when you call
I think it's the sound of a lament
and when you lament we think
it's the sound of an opened letter
and when I opened that letter
I heard your voice broken
in a new language.

We Were Cosmonauts

Before our departing flight

at the Moscow Airport,

I put my four-year-old

hand on my chest

and made a grand gesture,

pretending that the ache

emanating from my heart

would break me. Wailing

the only words in English

that I knew: *Oh, God!*

Oh, Pepsi! Oh, Cheerios! Oh, America!

My mother knew fewer words

than I did but she did know

Jewish and *refugee* and *immigrant*

and carried me onto the plane

midperformance and midhysteria.

My grandmother watching silently.

We were cosmonauts. My mother's

space suit: a full-length fur coat

worn over a full-length leather coat,

worn over every piece of jewelry she owned.

Traveling to outer space, the ultimate immigration.

We were aliens. Stepping off the plane

to find our sponsors, Barbara and Dan.

Matching sweaters and blue jeans,

handing us a prayer book and playing

Ace of Base in their minivan as they

drove us to the part of town

where they put all of the aliens.

That first night sleeping on the floor,

this planet sounding exactly like a woman

weeping into her pillow. Or maybe it was

my mother that was weeping, or maybe my mother was

the moon. Or maybe it was the hum of the laundromat

next door, where I would steal quarters

to play Tetris. A game invented

in that godless country

where you shape pieces

until they fit together

and once they find each other

they disappear.

Boris

There is an old can of tuna in my refrigerator
and I don't have the heart to throw it away
so I give it a name. I call it Boris. And sometimes
I think about Boris when I eat a ham sandwich
or when I frost a cake in lily white or when I wash
the dishes. When I have guests over I worry that they
will smell Boris, and how can I explain
why I won't throw him away? But he's in there
next to the eggs, and I imagine the refrigerator
alive in the twilight, and Boris pulling back his mouth
and singing to the fresh tuna, and how the young
don't believe in the old.

Marriage

Marriage is a lifelong commitment
to buy groceries for another person.
Each week. I buy you seven plums
because they are your morning ritual.
Every once in a while, you bring home
a bag of persimmons, and I slowly undress
them by the sink. We have not yet figured out
the right way to eat a pomegranate,
though the last time we were in Jerusalem
someone told me it was the forbidden fruit
and not the apple, which I am ashamed
to admit I almost never wash. I am unclean
in many ways, like the ham and cheese
Lunchable I hid from my grandmother,
or the turkey bacon that remarkably tastes like bacon
because maybe it is bacon. There is honesty
in the oatmeal but not the Greek yogurt
that was never eaten by the ancient Greeks, though
the wisdom of Aristotle
is printed on the side, *we are what we repeatedly do.*
You repeatedly standing in front of the milk.
Me repeatedly staring in the bbq aisle.
There are love poems everywhere,
but here in this breakfast pastry aisle
I hand you a box of Pop-Tarts
and say, "Put this in my toaster,"
and you know exactly what I mean.

Anecdote

I have spent years trying to cultivate a mature heart.
I read the appropriate books, I stare at artwork.
When I see a pendulum swing I make comments
about how the earth moves or how the
concept of time is a delightful notion or how
politics is common sense on fire. And what
a beautiful politician that red tulip would have been
but I cannot keep myself from laughing at an anecdote
about a beaver and his pile of wood, and how I made
a reference to a nipple in a poem once
and how Tolstoy must have felt when he believed
the devil to exist in his writing,
but I can't control you,
little red tulip.

Message from a Peeping Tom

This is a love poem.
Understand that my hands
are wrapped around my binoculars
and I dream about you in the present.

I am an anthropologist
studying mating habits
behind a rock in the middle
of the Serengeti, waiting
for the antelope to make
antelope love.
I don't have a degree, but I have visions.
I see a woman on the second floor
brushing her teeth in a macaroni
bowl moments before her boyfriend
gallops across the open plains.
I take notes, I keep charts.
When she collapses in the corner of her room
like a crumpled piece of paper, I worry.
Each night I bring tissues.
Each night they stay sealed in my bag.
Each night I whisper through these leaves in English.
But tonight allow me to seduce you in French.

Bonjour mon cheri.
Je voudrais une . . . hmm. I can't remember
anything else, but I can French kiss the tulip
curve of your mouth. Or I can feed you
the brie I have been aging in my cheese cellar,

saving fromage for this special occasion.
My darling,
I live in this tree.
I want nothing from you
and everything from you.
I watch you watch the spiders
weave patterns in your window.
I have two legs, but I can get more.
My darling I have eyes and legs
and binoculars, my darling this
is the poem I will leave on your doorstep:

I am standing in the middle
of the Louvre staring at
Chassériau's Esther.
Esther, you saved the Jews
from massacre, but as you
sit topless on your bed watching
television you look like
you couldn't care less
whether I lived or died.
You are the queen of the universe
unaware of her subjects
the stars.

Ornithology

Poets are not artists
because if you give a poet
an easel and a paint set
he will inevitably take his clothes off
and wait for the white space
to grow emaciated arms and paint
his likeness. I myself
have stared into the face of white space.
She is poorly fed and constantly drugged.
Pulling the shroud over her body
I followed a trail of letters to a house
in the forest. Language is essentially
what shows up when you place the poet
in an X-ray machine. The sternum made of q's and u's
and the ribcage an interlocked system
of vowel sounds. The logic is of course
complete bull a-e-i-o-u shit
but who doesn't love
a leap of faith. I have watched
exactly twenty-five birds
fly by my window in my lifetime
and each one of them proves
the existence of poetry.

1. A lark
2. A sparrow
3. An eagle
4. A rocking chair
5. A blue bird

6. A bluer bird

7. A bird who just feels blue

8. The unnamed

9. The unsayable

10. Everything that flies except things named flies

11. A fly

12. A baby dressed like a penguin

13. A penguin dressed like a baby

14. The grown man penguin

15. The zookeeper

16. The moment you felt thirst

17. What makes the branches ache

18. You, dear reader

19. A helicopter

20. The propelling of bodies in space

21. A rising phoenix

22. The crest of time

23. The molting sun

24. The birdcage of sound

25. A duck

What Is True for Birds

To get from Europe to the southernmost tip of Africa
you have to lose a part of your brain.
You are an apple in the sky,
take a bite out of your abdomen,
lose a quarter of your intestines.
We need just enough of the body
to fly. I can shave off
all of my hair, I can pluck out
these feathers, I can lose a kidney
or a pancreas. The ancient Egyptians
put the organs
of their lovers into jars.
If you break sarcophagus down
it means flesh-eating-stone.

And there you are
standing in your kitchen.
Throw away your dead irises
and put what is left of this
goldfinch into your beautiful mouth.

Psalm for Odessa

1.

Grandfather stuck between two genocides on the Black Sea
and you *innocent like clean bread,*
you ironed flat, without wrinkle,
you filling the darkness
the way a firefly fills a tightly closed jar
and dead the next morning.

2.

The inevitable truth that exists in every crowded room
that we are containers of imagination . . .
in my chest a barrel of plums
writing poems about the jam factory
and all the ways to be human.

3.

Adam names the rat a rat,
the rat a creature of survival,
it will eat through you if it has to.
Lot eating dinner with his wife
after she has turned to salt.
Lot whispering against the silence

Oh, Dearest God,
Oh, holiest phantom
I will break off her earlobe
I will split open this temple
I will eat my own heart.

4.

Turn around and look back at Odessa

5.

I return to her.

6.

Odessa, Oh, mother of color
and sorrow, your children
black and white and gray and blue.
We fight each other
in your streets and in your homes.
We put holes in your walls
but you forgive us everything

7.

A poplar tree grows out of your tenth story
window.

8.

Looking for grandfather, I am lost
in a communist cemetery. Officers and soldiers
beneath rusted tablets covered with flowers.
Later, I find myself in a Jewish cemetery,
rusted tablets covered with stones.

9.

After years of letters
God has returned to Odessa.
Finding it difficult to kneel
on tired knees, unaware of custom.

10.

The sun sets over the Black Sea
and the gangsters of the city
engrave this picture on their bodies.

On the right day you find the soul
of the gangster the cleanest of all.
On the right day you find a dead man
selling you raspberries.

Because government officials don't know what to do
with the dead and the hungry
they send both of them to market.

11.

There is one sad Georgian and one happy Georgian
and they are married.
She sings late into the night, and he sits
on a chair and watches her.
He holds her coat and walks her home,
washes her feet outside of their home
as she holds the oil lamp. It is too dark
to see anything. There is one
sad Georgian and one happy
Georgian in Odessa.

12.

Daughters of Odessa are often told
the history of good wives
when men sleep in strange beds
and women hang wet sheets to dry.

13.

Today it is quiet in Odessa and
every sailor knows a storm
is coming and no one knows
what to do but rearrange magnets
in the shapes of ships
and whisper to the refrigerator
save us.

14.

The storm unties his shoes.

15.

There is a prostitute in Odessa
and her name is Voskreseniye.
Which means Sunday,
which means resurrection of Christ.

16.

Underneath the skirts of Odessa,
there are petticoats and ruffles
of the French and German styles,
catacombs in between layers of lace,
a tunnel that a hand can slide down,
a space someone can run through, or a mouse.
Running away from darkness into darkness,
no one knows how deep it all goes.
Drop a coin down her dress
and only a mouse with a broken tail falls out.
Press your ear against her bodice
and you hear thousands of pairs of shoes.

Find the right tunnel and you end at the Eiffel Tower,
find the right tunnel and you end in Buchenwald.
Find the right tunnel and you end
in the middle of a dying star.
In the middle of a black galaxy, in the middle
of the Black Sea.

17.

Inside every plum.

18.

The black sea.

19.

I am standing naked before a mirror
and in the market there is a man standing
naked before a cow he has just butchered.
One of us is wearing an apron, one of us
a necklace with the hand of God
and one of us lies on a table,
her breasts torn open in the sun.

PART 2

American Radiance

New Eden

You know the movie where cell phones
become sentient and mankind is enslaved
through a series of poorly closed gates
and missed phone calls? The one where
it all somehow comes down to a cowboy
named Freedom Rings propelling in slow motion
toward an important red button.
The one that ends with a new dawn
and a new age for humans.

We should, of course, burn it all
and start again.
If we forget about trousers and T-shirts
we can reinvent them.
We can remerge from our caves
and find a new way to touch one another:
let me hold your ear
let me kiss your ankle
let me press my face against the side of your back
and make a farty suction noise as a way to say hello,
and repeat this action against the armpit
as a way to say goodbye.
And because of this, we will rarely say goodbye.
We will stand across from each other
arms up and pantless.
We will stand in our nakedness in awe of our new Eden.
But this time we will throw away the fig leaves
and cover ourselves in bubble wrap,

spending long evenings popping
each other's cloaks by candlelight,
ashamed again at our magnificence, terrified
of our own knowledge.
And when it will be time to express adoration
we will use the words borrowed
from our ancestors whose broken records
we found in the rubble.
Holding each other among shattered bricks
and electronic fossils,
we'll whisper the new way to say I love you:
doo-wop, doo-wop, shoo-bop, shoo-bop

Adoration

Svetlana was named Svetlana
because she adored the light
and when I say adored
I mean truly the word adoration
because we've lost what it means
to be truly devoted to something.
We say we love our families
or our countries or our ideas
but I know a man who fell
in love with a little purple plum.
He carried her in his pocket.
He knew everything about that plum.
And you might say, but what is there to know
about a piece of fruit? And that's why
you can't fall in love. That's why the light
has become just another reflection
of your own sensibility. And you
rip plums wide open
and toss the beating hearts.

Raptor

After the destruction of Jewish cemeteries in Philadelphia and St. Louis

My grandmother wants a bird
on her grave
and I say wants not wanted
because she is still alive
flipping through the "tasteful tombstones" catalogue.

To be clear—
there are twenty-five different birds
you can place on top of yourself
when you die. Yes, there are the predictably
delicate doves and symbolic sparrows
but my grandmother is interested
in something more predatory.

The hawk kills with its claws,
the falcon mouth first.
The martial will snap a man's arm
in half, and a Steller can consume
a baby seal. There are five types of eagles
that will "steal your toddler."

When they cleared out her village
in 1941, my grandmother survived
by jumping on a train to the mountains,
her mother and mother's mother
buried birdless back in Ukraine.

My grandmother now
shaking in her gold cardigan
and lifting her arms up
toward the Kansas sky.
Winged raptor. Feathered Moses.
Resurrected and in rage.

Translating Ashes

I was not born good but
in the likeness of my father.
A man full of ashes
who loved tanks as a boy
and knew life through a dream.
I too was inflicted like a dog
with the disease of dreams,
reaching my hand into a fish tank
believing I could talk to the animals.
And as a child I spoke to the fireflies
their bodies broken with radiance
the cracks of my body
full of light until I became a woman.
My flesh with the other flesh
my mouth in this shape
you in a language I can never touch.

Crane Fly

It was days before I saw him again,
body broken on a golden dish,
legs propped in the air.
He stayed there a long time.
I peeled a pear in his honor,
left the rind in the sink
and watched the fruit flies
hover like hummingbirds.
And I think of my crane fly,
legs too long, wings
like a cheap kite wobbling
and unsure of the wind.
Like the man I watched
for twenty years
find his way down
the staircase every day,
legs crushed against the bed
frame, the air he stood on,
my crane fly, my king Midas.

Rasputin and Alexei

Dear child, you lose her
with every falling staircase.
You want to be a man
holding your grandfather's cross
saw, the blade even longer than Olga
with her boots on. You want to saw
her braids off. You want to make a rope
and escape out of the window. You
want to be lighter than air,
a bird who doesn't bleed.
You want to be a white cloud,
you want to be this feather I have
pulled from my beard, floating
from this shallow grave. You
want so many things.

Moscow 1972

We could have bought some land,
that's what the other guy did—
he grew tulips on his and became a rich man
sending the beauty out of Russia
but I wanted to see the world so I bought a Volga
and drove to Moscow in the storm.
In Russia, the storm was white
and you were quiet, having seen the world
thirty years ago, a young man then, walking
through the snow. When the car broke
down and you slaughtered a rabbit
for dinner it was the only time
I ever saw you kill.

Deaf Sonnet, Глухой Сонет

Для Исаак

There is no room for elegy in Brazos Bend.
There are no howler monkeys around
the banks where I wish to howl.
There is for this moment the red burrowing owl
scowling at the shovel where I plant this memory—
grandfather shattering every cognac glass
and singing with his uncaged body
the many names of stars that spill
like spiders out of the pupils of dogwoods
that look and are silent against the beating
of the freshwater drum. There is no music left
only the sound of broken images. Inside
my sonnet, this trombone and this accordion flower
that blooms, unfurls his petals, and in his nakedness sighs.

Firefly

I do not agree with the way the hydrangea blossoms.
When they rip open in the spring I walk right by them.
I know they are there, but I do not believe in their stink.
It reminds me of something, maybe
what was once my own humanity, perhaps
too much I know how it hurts,
like how many insects had to die
before their own bodies
began to burn in the night.

Boot

Hello, Constantine,
not the great Roman emperor
but the little Russian boy
who sits on a stool in his father's
shoe repair shop
watching his fingers turn
to leather and finding long laces
to wrap around his small ankles,
his quiet hands.

Trawler

My body ages every day
which is a form of intimacy
like you pulling the blue crab
from the tentacles of a sea nettle,
telling stories about Odysseus
and the shape of war,
the cannon dive of the pelican,
shrimp, shrapnel, ectoplasm of fog
and gray memory, our boat made
of pink cerebellum and coral
appendages, the sea too big to fit
into the barrel of a gun and too small
to fill the space between guilt
and evening mourning. Our church
is surrounded by dolphins who know
nothing of our tragedy, and through this
they bring their priestly comfort.

Spicer's Promise to Lorca

that *the loneliness always returns*
the warmth of body leaves us,
we lose so much we are unaware of—

two hands that wash the cherries in the kitchen
two feet that want nothing more than the Earth
elbows that were never appreciated
though there was once a civilization
who worshipped their hinge,
knuckles that pop with unimaginable pleasure
the larynx that you were convinced was a mythical
animal, the imagination which is housed
like a ship in the navel
the brain, an old Philco radio
transmitting to the stars

and every year on August 5th
the *Curiosity* rover stops collecting data
and sings himself Happy Birthday
Happy birthday
you miserable machine
you beautiful human
you shepherd of the rocks.

Spud Love

I have loved you
like a potato,
dropping out of backpacks
lying on the ground,
asking to be grated
or boiled in a tub.

Loyal these eyes,
my love could power
a small battery or a light bulb.

Potato love is patient,
lying in a dark cellar,
a grocery bin, the farmer's
wagon, the palm of his hands.
The man who peeled me
to the bone.

In the Moonlight

The heads, they follow me.
Not political or villainous
metaphors for power, no, these are
thinking human heads heavy
in my backpack that drop to the ground
like potatoes. You see they tend to show up.
Yesterday I opened my locker
and a redhead dropped to the ground;
I was embarrassed to say the least.
Perhaps it is all a figment of my imagination
and if I close my eyes they will disappear.
Except, I still see you behind the shutters
legs crossed on the love seat stroking
a beautiful head of hazelnut hair. I beg you
to stop, but you are a poem
smoking your long cigarette, taunting me
with my grandmother's necklace or the basement
full of sparrows you unleash at inopportune moments.
I remember when you fed them rice and they exploded
like fire sparklers in midair, the lovers in mid-stanza
covered in bird feces and feathers.
I remember how beautiful the sea was that night
we got into the glass-bottom boat. How the angel
fish swam in circles in the moonlight, how horrified
I was when we cast back our nets and found a crab
pinching the nose of a head not unlike yours.

Spilling

When I say insect
I do not mean
the body that is crawling
across this page
but instead I mean
the many legs
of my longing,
each one a love letter
that only consists of one
letter, you
and you
and the space
between breaths
that fills every conversation
up to the brim.

Breasts

My breasts are like Aristotle and Plato.
They never see eye to eye—
when I take them out to parties
they explain the nature of man
to anyone who will listen.
When I lie in bed at night
I hear them quarrel about
the allegory of the cave,
the joy of stupidity.
It would be nice in that cave,
huddled up in the darkness.
I'd be a little girl again
the philosophers gone,
my chest covered in cave paintings—
what beasts they would draw.

Into the Blackberry

When he walked from Odessa
to Budapest he passed fields
of clothes and empty shoes,
wildflowers growing through buttons,
between zippers, butterflies unfurling
their wings and the smell
of meat in spring.

When he came back he found Vera
in a basement, her hair to the floor,
broken like a dozen eggs.
I count the ants
in the fruit bowl
and I wonder
the way children do
about what heaven is
and what it is
that holds me back
from sticking my head
into the blackberry.

When I remember my childhood
I see the shrapnel in his flesh
and the bodies of mice
dancing in the walls,
dandelion growing
in a pair of abandoned
shoes, and how I slowly learned
about the quiet horror.

Records of Failed Weapons of World War II

I have trained these dogs to run
after tanks like children
chasing ice cream trucks.
This one ran faster than the others,
she knew how fear smelled in the damp
spring. I watched her paws on fire,
I wrote Dear God in the record books.

Or consider the World War
II scientist playing with his toys
in the bathtub, dreaming
of aircraft carriers made of ice
and sawdust. I dream
of airplanes sawed out of ice blocks,
melting like Icarus
in the dandelion sun.

I imagine the man of wind tickled
at the sight of the wind cannon
shooting breath at unsuspecting pigeons
and weeping when he saw the invisible
man of air killed as a casualty,
surrounded in a pool of oxygen,
oxygen everywhere.

This city is made of paper,
fold enough sheets
to build a house,
fly a paper airplane.
This bat is strong enough
to carry her child in flight,
here is a bomb. Here is a city,
here is a fire, here is a mother
burning her wings, here is a bomb
where she once felt the weight
of wrinkled body. Here is a baseball,
hold it in your palm
and watch the forest disappear.

Rumi in the Mouth of the Snake

Your grandparents were wild rats,
dancing between the walls
of the kitchen, feasting on cheeses
and cognac, bathing in the filth
behind Madame Bovary's Bistro,
vacationing in garbage dumps,
making love the way rats do,
in rat positions with their rat tails
tingling like radio antennas
as messages from god pour
directly into their souls,
the rat soul so quiet and hungry
as were the first angels.
You think of them now,
staring into the eyes of the snake.
You think of your sister
no bigger than a tulip bulb,
reciting Rumi in the moment
before they pulled your body
out of the tank and into the darkness
you mustn't be afraid of death,
you're deathless soul you
can't be kept in a dark grave.
You think of rat heaven,
streets lined with cake crumbs,
the clouds porous, the sun
just a giant wheel of cheese.

The first rats in Eden welcome
you with apple cores.
The mother you never knew
silver haired and weeping,
speaks in a broken tongue,
God has decreed life for you
and he will give another
and another and another,
you are my ninetieth son
come join me with your eighty-nine
brothers, and sisters, and brothers.

Poem for the Man Playing Piano
in Front of the Wall of Police

Kiev, 2014

This was the song your mother would hum:
da de du da, du du du da.
She once took you to the zoo in Odessa
and you watched an elephant
paint a picture of an elephant
and everyone laughed
but you stood there in your silence.
When they told you the storm was over
in the middle of the storm
your clothes began to stain.
Rain is the sound of a violin. A storm
is symphony. You hear it now.
Last week lightning struck Christ
the Redeemer and the papers exploded
with proclamations of the end
and the beginning. When your fingers break
you can still cup your hands into a prayer.
It was how your mother taught you that God speaks silently,
that when Babel fell silence was the answer.
You sit here on your piano stool
in front of the wall of police,
silence erupting all around you,
closer to God than you'd ever dreamed.

Cremation

Teach me how to sing
the childhood song
where we scream
about ashes and we all
fall down.

In Odessa, the dead walk
the streets and the living watch
from behind closed gates.

My grandmother hid
in that basement there. Here
hell is fire, grandfather
sent to Siberia. Years of hard labor
bring people closer to God.

Heaven is full of convicts
with broken backs.
After chopping wood
for twenty years ask for fire.

Your door is made
from wood, press your ear
against it and listen to the sound
a hatchet makes.

If you wake up in a world of ash
remember you have reached
God in your own way.
Cumulonimbus, cirrus, stratus
once had eyes like you.

This Was His Garden

Crouching on the heels of my feet
I tug at the whiskers of a radish
and pull a clown nose
out of the soil.
Placing the radish on my face
I turn my lips downward
pretending I am not unlike
the clown at the circus
driving a miniature car,
stopping dramatically in
center stage,
opening the passenger door
and waiting for something,
anything, a dog bouncing on a pogo
stick, an elephant with garlands
of marigolds, a ballerina with
cotton candy bursting
from her hips, a tiny girl balancing
a baton on her head, exactly
one million butterflies with synchronized
movements or at least one million
human beings dressed like butterflies flapping
their wings in unison. A trumpet, an oboe,
a hamburger, something between pieces of bread.
But as I stand in front of the open car door
nothing comes out, the tiny car is a void
and the audience is furious.
My grandfather was buried there,
and the audience is furious.

American Radiance

Walmart, 1992

There is a radiance
the way the firefly
breaks his body
and you stand in the shadows
of that light,
small, born of things.

*

In the Soviet market
you find ways to break
the line. Six years old and
radiant you run with
tomatoes heavy in your pockets.
Today, there are turnips,
tomorrow, fresh dill.
If you are determined enough
you will eventually make
a salad or an escape.

*

Walmart is full of objects
that make everything better.
In the Home Improvement
section you can improve your home.
Install light switches in rooms that do
not need light switches
just to feel what it is like to

have the momentary power
of Let There Be Light. Let
there be a sale on candles
that not only burn but do so
beautifully. In my bones
I know there is no such thing
as an actual cucumber melon
but I smell it with such certainty.
Here, everything is better with objects.
That tightness in your chest
when you think of home
only needs a humidifier
that will make the air so soft
you'll think your lungs are full
of silkworms. You can buy spools
of satin to remind you of your
grandmother's gloves that touched
your tear-stained face at the airport.
Would you ever come back?
The answer is no. Even when
you came back.

*

In the produce section
you try to make sense
of every single fruit. But
beyond the obvious passion fruit
or plum, you know you really

loved home with the simplicity
of a piece of bread. What wouldn't
you have done for it? The squeaky
wheels of your cart telling you
to fill yourself with things
you don't need but can't live without.
Now twenty-six years
in this store, in this country.
The moment you stand
in an aisle of lamps
and believe in the darkness.

IN THE PRAIRIE SCHOONER BOOK PRIZE IN POETRY SERIES

To order or obtain more information on these or other University of Nebraska Press titles, visit nebraskapress.unl.edu.